Net Profit Workbook

Seven Steps to Your Most Profitable Year

By: Max Keller

www.CustomersChasingYou.com – info@saviorpublishinghouse.com – 817-527-8207

Net Profit Workbook

Seven Steps to Your Most Profitable Year

ISBN: 978-1-7338459-7-7

2140 Hall Johnson Ste. 102-320

Grapevine, TX 76051

Disclaimer

The information in this book is not meant to replace the advice of a certified professional. Please consult a licensed advisor in matters relating to your personal and professional well-being including your mental, emotional and physical health, finances, business, legal matters, and education. The views and opinions expressed throughout the book are those of the author and do not necessarily reflect the views or opinions of any other agency organization, employer, publisher, or company. Since we are criticality-thinking human beings, the views of the author are always subject to change at any time. Any references to past performance may not be indicative of future results. No warranties or past performance may not be indicative of future results. No warranties or guarantees are expressed or implied by the publisher's choice to include any of the content in this volume.

If you choose to attempt any of the methods mentioned in this book, the author and publisher advise you to take full responsibility for your results. The author and publisher are not liable for any damages or negative consequences from any treatment, action, application, or preparation to any person reading or following the information in this book.

Table of Contents

Acknowledgements

This book would not have been possible without the outstanding clients, teachers, coaches, mentors, and business partners I have had the pleasure to work with. Thank you for your support – Max Keller

Introduction

Goal of workbook

The goal of this book is to enable members to experience **three major, quantitative, net-profit events** in their business this year, as a direct result of:

1. Information
2. Tools
3. Accountability

Seven steps to your most profitable year

In following this seven-step process members will experience three, major, quantitative events:

1. Create your one-year finish line (reverse engineer the net profit).
2. Identify your starting line (how close are you now?).
3. What other opportunities and risks are you missing? (Are you choosing the right vehicle? What risks are hiding in the shadows?). Identify the biggest obstacle in the way (what is blocking your path to success?).
4. Discover the hurdles getting in the way of your progress.

5. Identify the main issues at the core of your business's symptoms (instead of saying "sales are not enough", change the conversation to "why are sales not higher?" What is the root cause reason you don't have more sales?
6. Create a one-year strategy playbook to get you to the finish-line (daily, weekly, and monthly steps; when, what, how, who?).
7. Execute the three biggest profit opportunities for your business this year (take accountability for the calls you make).

Notes:

____

____

____

____

____

Two journey choices

There are two paths to choose from in the completion of this profit journey:

Road 1 - on your own.

- It will be up to you to complete the workbook.
- You will need to process and identify the key information.
- Complete the tools to a high level of precision.
- Hold yourself accountable, not to your goals, but to the non-negotiable jobs you must do in your business.
- Issue consequences to yourself when you allow outside influences to get in the way of your daily, weekly, and monthly non-negotiable activities.

Road 2 - with your Profit Coach

- You will be held accountable by your profit coach, to complete the workbook.
- The profit coach will help you identify the key information for your business.
- The coach will help you learn how to use the tools to a high level of precision.
- The coach will hold you accountable for your goals and non-negotiables.

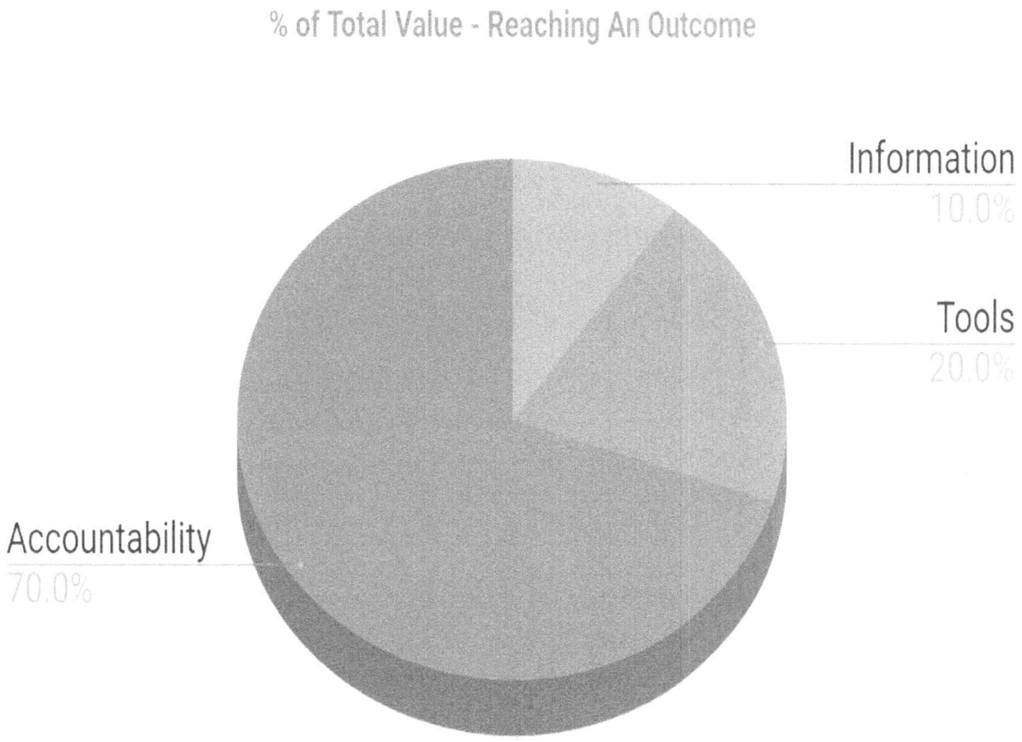

Who will the workbook benefit?

Busy real-estate professionals, who spend more time putting out fires and not enough time creating a conducive environment for reflective thinking about the root causes of the problems and symptoms.

Who is this Book <u>not</u> for?

This book is **not** for the business owner that says they want to promote changes and then falls back into old habits. This is **not** for the business owner that makes decisions that directly contradict with increasing net profit. This book is **not** for the business owner that is too busy to focus on this framework. If you think any of the above describe you, please pass this book on and best of luck in your journey this year.

This book is not for those who don't answer their phone, don't return calls, or don't follow through on what they say they will do.

Current challenges

We gathered feedback from current members during the design process of both this book and the program, and some of the key challenges they face were identified as:

- Lower margins;
- Lack of clarity;
- Thinking of their principal goals in less time than it takes to order a take-out, and with the absence of a clear process;
- Not calculating the risks involved with their strategies or plans;
- Encountering too many fixed expenses;
- Too much local real estate cycle exposure;
- Struggling to review financial data quickly each month;
- Lack of trend analysis;
- Not hiring the top talent in the marketplace.

Notes:

___

___

Desired results

Our goal is for the implementor (you and your team) of this book to have at least three large incremental net profit events in a 12-month period. The amount of the net profit event will have to do with how closely you follow the steps, the size of your business, and many other factors. We cannot guarantee success for anyone but feel confident focusing on net profit can lead to tremendous results. Greater net profit may not solve all problems, but it is a lifeline that provides owners with compensation for their risk and the breathing room to make use of their most powerful tool: Thinking.

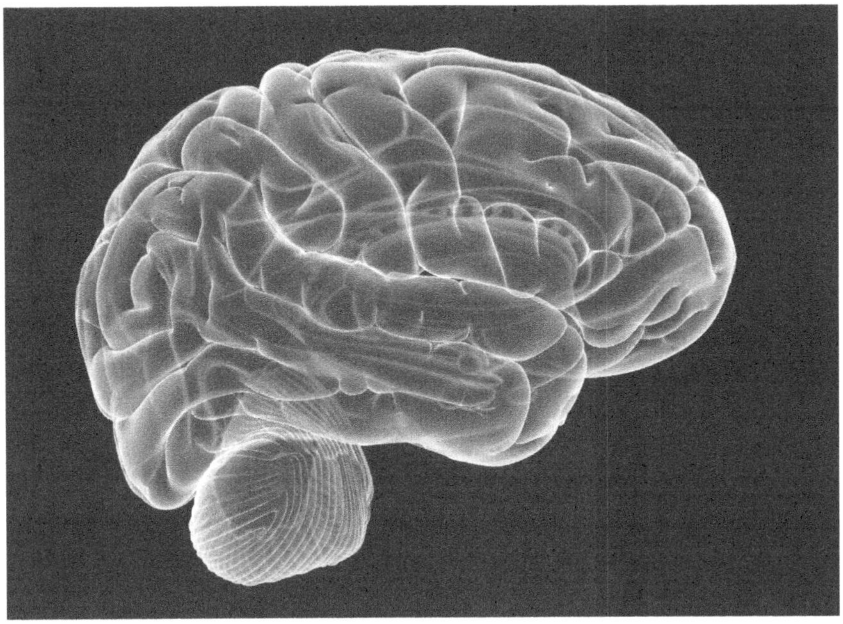

How Much Time Are You Investing Each Week Using This?

Our focus

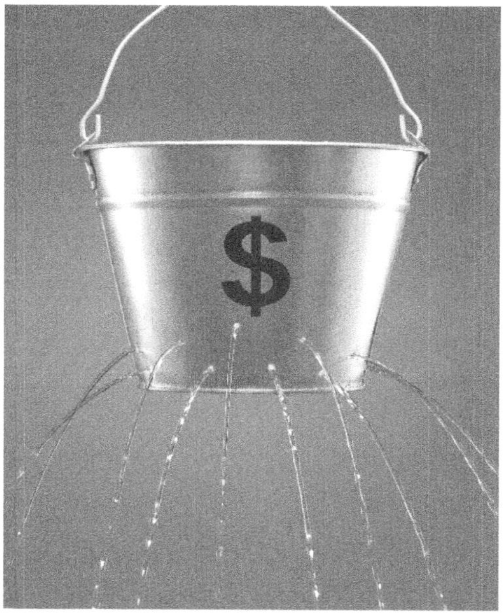

We focus on helping real estate business who want to attract more customers and become more profitable. Most of our members have between 1 – 20 employees. These investors have a minimum of three years' experience and are looking for a way to consistently boost profits margins, unlock real estate profits, and are finding it difficult to release time for planning.

How much money are you left with on the table? Be a conduit instead of a holey bucket. This system allows you to plug the holes draining your profits, so you can bestow more blessings to your family and others. Do you know how much money you are losing at this moment? Can you make and lose money at the same time? You can: You probably are, and it needs to stop. You are our focus.

How this system delivers results

We have the steps you are not currently, or consistently applying that will transport you to the profit finish line. This proprietary system utilizes practices most people are not taking advantage of and, if followed, is the path to your profit goals.

The ultimate goal is for members to achieve clarity on what the biggest opportunities and risks in their business are; selecting the best strategies to achieve their goals; and that they are held accountable to one the **results** alone. This workbook is for the attainment of profit **results** and if this is what you want, you need to invest in the system.

The approach we take in this program is different to those you may be used to. After working with countless companies in our field, our team has:

- Observed crucial opportunities that have been missed;
- Identified and eliminated timewasters;
- Increased focus in core areas;
- Established a net profit goal (vs. a revenue goal);
- Selected precise profit activities (how the money will be made);
- Made accurate assumptions and used these to drive the numbers;
- Selected and applied the right strategies to hit the numbers;
- Broken the year into quarters, and each quarter into monthly goals, with a focus on results instead of effort.

For the members to experience success they will need to change their belief systems from being overscheduled and diluted, to a simple and more focused business strategy that facilitates the attainment of bigger goals.

What does your company do? Is it working?

There are just three things that every company does:

1. Lead generation,
2. Lead conversion,
3. Product and service.

Profit Levers - there is only a small number of things that affect profit:

1. Leads,
2. Conversion rate,
3. Average transactions,
4. Average price,
5. Profit margin.

"Are we providing 5% value to 100% of the people, or 100% value to 5% of the people?"

– Max Keller

The process—what do you need to do to get results?

Activity	Hours	Description
Time Investment One-Time	7	Hours
Monthly Hours	2	Monthly Investment
Total One-Year Time Investment	31	Total Hours
Incremental Profit Goal	$30,000	Gross Profit
Total One-Year Incremental Profit Goal	$90,000	Gross Profit
Projected Profit / Time Invested	**$2,903**	Per Hour
Working Hours Per Year (40x50)	2000	Total Work Hours
Net Profit Hours / Total Work Hours	**1.55%**	% of Work Hours

Thinking sessions

- Plan at least one of these per week.
- 30 minutes.
- Select a question from the following pages that is often on your mind. What is your biggest challenge right now?
- Find an area free of distractions.
- Write the question down on a piece of paper and begin to think of possible solutions.
- When the session is up, review your list and look at the top three items you wrote that you can act on.
- If you need more time focusing on this issue, schedule the same question again.

"If I had an hour to solve a problem, I'd spend 55 minutes thinking about the problem and 5 minutes thinking about solutions."

– Albert Einstein

Chapter 1 – Creating a Finish Line

"Make sure every day you do what matters most. When you know what matters most, everything makes sense. When you don't know what matters most, anything makes sense."

— Gary Keller, ***The One Thing: The Surprisingly Simple Truth Behind Extraordinary***

Part 1 – Pre-Planning

- What will my plan measure?

- Where do I want the business to be at the end of year?

- Am I creating goals or just wishful thinking?

- The goal needs to have a specific designation where the progress can be tracked.

- Am I trying to be everything to everyone or a foundational source to a niche group?

Part 2 – Planning

- How small is the target I am aiming at?

- My plan is to make __________ profit by _________ (date) by doing:

- What outcome or goal is my number one priority? Why?

Part 3 – Reflecting

- How much time am I investing each day in thinking about where I am headed?

- Is my plan deliberately vague, because I am afraid to commit to a specific plan of action?

- Am I setting the same goals each year, but never hitting them?

"A VISION is a precise, clearly defined goal with a detailed plan and timetable for achieving that goal."

— Steven K. Scott, *The Richest Man Who Ever Lived: King Solomon's Secrets to Success, Wealth, and Happiness*

Chapter 2 – Identifying Your Starting Line

"One of the major differences between successful and unsuccessful people is that the former look for problems to resolve, whereas the latter make every attempt to avoid them."

— Grant Cardone, *The 10X Rule: The Only Difference Between Success and Failure*

Setting goals is important but knowing where you are today is the only way to start creating the right plan.

Instead of thinking "we are really on track" or "business is booming" let's use this time to get really invested.

Part 1 – Clarity

- Do I have real clarity on where the business is today?

- If I asked my business how it was doing, what would it say?

- What part of my current story is fiction and what part is fact?

- What part of my business do I not like to talk about? Why?

- How do I know if my business is doing well? Is my business doing well?

- Am I being completely honest about reality?

- Am I being honest with myself about my real starting point and capacity?

- What have been the biggest changes in my business in the last three years? What have I done about them?

- If I could shut down my business today and totally start over, what would I keep? What would I change?

Part 2 – Time

- How much time am I investing each day in thinking about where my business is right now?

- How could I use my time more purposefully?

- How could my team use their time more purposefully?

- What are my biggest timewasters?

Part 3 – Energy

- What important actions are not consistently being done in my business?

- What am I doing each day that I shouldn't be? What am I not doing each day that I should be?

Part 4 – Money

- Is my business meeting customer expectations better, the same, or worse than when it started?

- Does this business add value to the current market?

- If I bought a business that is just like mine, how much would I pay for it?

- Instead of asking why I am not getting more customers, why are the customers I want to work with not choosing me? What can I do about it?

- Is this business a good business?

- What problems in my business never seem to go away? Why do they keep recurring?

- With our current customers and volume, why is my business not more profitable? What can I do about it?

- Are my overhead expenses helping attract new customers, keeping existing ones, or bringing in more referrals?

- Do customers refer people to my business? If not, why not?

Part 5 – Team

- What are my team's strengths?

- What are my team's weaknesses?

"Before success comes in any man's life, he is sure to meet with much temporary defeat, and, perhaps, some failure. When defeat overtakes a man, the easiest and most logical thing to do is to quit. That is exactly what the majority of men do. More than five hundred of the most successful men this country has ever known told the author their greatest success came just one step beyond the point at which defeat had overtaken them."

— Napoleon Hill, *Think and Grow Rich: The Landmark Bestseller Now Revised and Updated for the 21st Century*

Chapter 3 – Opportunities and Risks

"Stop thinking about business in terms of your selfish desires, whether it's money, dreams or "do what you love." Instead, chase needs, problems, pain points, service deficiencies, and emotions."

— M.J. DeMarco, *The Millionaire Fastlane*

Opportunity Filter – When a new opportunity comes your way, do you always say "Yes" or "Maybe"? Are you the victim of shiny objects syndrome? When a new opportunity comes your way, use the following system to assess whether it is truly an opportunity worth pursuing.

Answer the following series of questions honestly:

Does this new opportunity:

- Make more money?
- Take less of my time?
- Use less of my team's time?
- Have lower taxes (long term)?
- Include reoccurring revenue?
- Contain more control of the business risks?
- Have a larger scale (national vs local)?
- Seem more enjoyable?
- Have more leverage (Time, Money, Energy)?
- Contain less legal risk?

Use the filter on the last page to analyze profit potential to increase focus on the highest profit goals. If you take this opportunity, what are the risks? What could go wrong and what would that affect? Nothing happens in business in a vacuum. When you think about the risks associated with an opportunity, try to think about the cause and effect each risk will have further down the line, for all levels of your business.

"Essentialism: only once you give yourself permission to stop trying to do it all, to stop saying yes to everyone, can you make your highest contribution towards the things that really matter."

— Greg McKeown, *Essentialism: The Disciplined Pursuit of Less*

Part 1 – Money

Success with customers = what we are good at + what the customer needs:

- What is creating the void between where I want to be and where I currently am?

- Have I taken on too much debt?

- When I borrowed money in the past was it based on emotions or numbers? Where can I share equity, instead of debt, and spread out the risk?

- What are my customers' biggest challenges?

- What constitutes success for my customers?

- Do I have the right solutions for my customers?

- What information are my customers missing?

- What is the biggest challenge my customers currently experience?

- What are the gaps in the services I (or my competitors) provide and what my customers want?

Part 2 – Time

- How much time each day am I investing in thinking about opportunities and risks in my business?

- How much time each day do I spend communicating via phone, text, or email?

- How many minutes each day do I spend in a completely distraction-free area, thinking about the questions in this book?

- How many minutes a day do I spend in a completely distraction-free area, reading?

- How many minutes a day do I spend totally free of distractions?

- What will my customers' expectations be 12 months from now?

- In the last two years, when have I chased something that has damaged a part of my business that was working well? Why do I have 'shiny object syndrome'?

Part 3 – Team

- Does my business have a culture that creates opportunities, or risks?

- Does my team make me look better or worse than I am?

- If I lost this person, _______________, my business would be in trouble. What can I do about that?

- Am I asking the right people for advice?

Part 4 – Taxes

- What can I do to lower my business' tax burden?

Part 5 – Recurring Revenue

- How much could I sell my business for today?

- What services would my customers pay for monthly?

Part 6 – Risks

- Am I feeling the impact of unknown risks right now?

- Am I only focusing on opportunities and ignoring the risks?

- Is this profit margin worth the time, effort, and risk?

- If my business is only concentrated in one area, what happens if my business model no longer fits that area?

- How could technology and innovation disrupt my current business? Is it already happening?

- What are the risks and possible impacts, if this new opportunity does not work out the way I expect? How long will it take to feel the repercussions?

- Is the product or service I provide a good one, or am I just hoping someone will like it? Why is the targeted marketing audience saying no to my business? Don't assume, ask them.

Part 7 – Scale

- What problems am I best equipped to solve right now (list up to five)?

- Which of these has the biggest need and gap in services provided by competing businesses?

Part 8 - Enjoyment

- Am I actively engaged in my business? Am I delegating or abdicating?

- Over the past two years, which customers were the most profitable and which were the best to work with?

- What did these customers all have in common and is my marketing currently attracting my ideal customers?

Part 9 – Leverage

- Can I solve any problem there is in all businesses around the world, in the US, or in my local area?

Part 10 - Legal

- What potential risks are there that could result in my business being sued? What damage could this do to my business?

Final Thoughts

When you think about a new opportunity, remember it is not in a vacuum. In order to take advantage of an opportunity a business system must be set up and executed around it. Remember: Hope is not a strategy.

Ask yourself:

What are the resources needed to facilitate the running of my business?

How long is the ramp-up period?

What are the profit opportunities?

Does this contribution reward myself, or the investors?

"I insist on a lot of time being spent thinking, almost every day, to just sit and think. That is very uncommon in American business. I read and think. So, I do more reading and thinking, and make fewer impulse decisions than most people in business. I do it because I like this kind of life."

– Warren Buffett

Chapter 4 – Hurdles

"And what makes people work is an idea worth working for, along with a clear understanding of what needs to be done."

— Michael E. Gerber, *The E-Myth Revisited: Why Most Small Businesses Don't Work and What to Do About It*

Without understanding what is holding us back, we can't create a plan that will help us overcome them consistently. Afterall, if there were nothing holding you back, you would already be there.

Part 1 – Clarity

- What is holding me back, or blocking my path, from where I am to where I want to be? (This must be clearly defined before you can move on to the next step).

- What is the biggest hurdle causing problems in my business?

- How long has this hurdle been there and how does it block my business from progressing?

- If I hired someone else to run my business, what changes would they make?

- What are the three biggest risks my business is facing right now?

- What would the impact of these risks be? What is the likelihood of them happening? Do I have control over whether they happen?

Part 2 – Time

- How much time each day am I investing in thinking about the hurdles my business faces?

- Am I skimming off the bottom 20% of customers each year? Am I creating ways to retain the top 20% of customers each year? Do I know who my top and bottom customers are?

Part 3 – Energy

- What are the questions that no-one is asking?

- What questions explore the problems deeper?

Part 4 – Money

- Why do I want to grow my company? Am I bored? DO I think it's the only direction I can go in?

- How can I make more money with the level of customers I currently have?

Part 5 – Team

- What must change about the working day and culture to eliminate or overcome this hurdle?

- What can my team do to transition from a fire-drill office to an efficient and methodical office?

- When have my team let process maps and procedures impede the service we provide our customers?

- What can I delegate to other members of my team?

Final Thoughts

Prospects that hinder your progress, do so intentionally. Find out why and then think about what you can do about it:

1. Improve your product or service.
2. Target a more ideal customer for your services.

"Losing money comes down to two things… Something happened that was not supposed to happen … Something that was supposed to happen didn't happen"

-Keith Cunningham, *The Road Less Stupid*

Chapter 5 - Core Issues

"From a Christian perspective Jesus not only knew what these people needed, he could instantly heal them. But he didn't. Instead, he asked them to declare what they wanted. It seems their apparent need was not their greatest need. More than healing, they needed clarity."

— **Michael Hyatt,** ***Your Best Year Ever: A 5-Step Plan for Achieving Your Most Important Goals***

Part 1 – Clarity

- What is the real obstacle, or root cause, that is impeding my progress?

- What is the cause of the symptoms I am facing?

- Has my current business situation changed dramatically? Have I planned a pivot, or am I hoping things just turn around?

- When I identify other hurdles and symptoms, what is core issue driving them? What can I do to eliminate or minimize the cause?

- Has the market changed what my business needs to be today?

- Am I simply solving the business symptoms, or tackling the core issues behind the symptoms (core issues stick around until they are solved)?

- What is the main core issue in my business I need to solve?

- If business has taken a downturn, am I just trying to do more of the thing that is not working, or am I working to identify the core issue and planning how I can pivot my company?

- What keeps me up worrying late at night?

Part 2 – Time

- How much time each day do I invest thinking about core issues in my business?

- Too many time owners are slow in making changes when issues are affecting their business: Is my plan changing as quickly as it needs to?

- Am I really 100% committed to the business and the essential tasks that need to get done to achieve my goals, or am I just "playing" at being a business owner?

- Am I purposeful with how I invest my time?

- Am I constantly interrupted by my phone, email, or employees? How are these impeding my ability to think?

Part 3 – Energy

- Am I following my own scorecard for success or one someone else made for me?

- When I am having an important conversation with someone, in person, do I look at my phone if it rings or beeps? How do I decide where to direct my focus?

- Am I constantly distracted?

Part 4 – Money

- Are my overheads low and variable? Why not? Once money is spent it is gone forever.

- Do I have three months of cash reserves in the bank? What about six months?

- Why are my customers saying no to my business? Is it because my service is not right for them? Is it that my company is difficult to work with? Is it because my customers do not understand how much better my company is than the competition?

- When a customer buys from me, are they 99.9% sure my service or product will solve their problem? What level of confidence do customers have in my company?

Part 5 – Team

- What is preventing my employees from being more successful?

- What core issues have I been putting off addressing with my team?

Final Thoughts

Think strategic, not tactical. Tactical provides medicine for the symptoms, without addressing the core issue. Strategic thinking explores why the symptoms are there in the first place and doesn't stop until the core issue is identified and corrected.

Instead of: How can I double my net profit this year?

Ask: Why is my business not twice as profitable? What core issues are holding my business back?

If you create a finish-line plan that solves the symptoms of a core issue without resolving the core issues, you will feel better, but the success will be short-lived. When the core issue rears its head again you will be back in the same position, only this time it will be worse, because you will have already wasted resources on the symptoms. Create a finish-line plan that focuses on eliminating the hurdles and core issues.

"The Deep Work Hypothesis: The ability to perform deep work is becoming increasingly rare at exactly the same time it is becoming increasingly valuable in our economy. As a consequence, the few who cultivate this skill, and then make it the core of their working life, will thrive."

— Cal Newport, *Deep Work: Rules for Focused Success in a Distracted World*

Chapter 6 – Creating a Playbook

"Discomfort brings engagement and change. Discomfort means you're doing something that others were unlikely to do, because they're hiding out in the comfortable zone. When your uncomfortable actions lead to success, the organization rewards you and brings you back for more."

— Seth Godin, *Linchpin: Are You Indispensable?*

Steps to increase your profits

Are you always in a hurry to add new leads to a broken business process? Before you start increasing the direct mail budget, make sure you have asked yourself the following questions first (in order):

- Am I keeping my customers?

- Can I sign up customers for a recurring sale, such as membership?

- Are my existing customers recommending me and sending me new customers?

- Do my customers think I can solve their problems?

- What is my sales process like?

- What is my lead conversion rate?

- Can I sell other products and services to my existing customers?

- Can I bring in more leads to our company (if you bring more leads in before you look at the other areas first, you are going to waste money)?

Part 1 – Pre-planning

- How will I achieve the goal I set in the first chapter?

- How do I design an easy-to-follow plan that has all the actions I need to achieve my business goals?

- Are there B Team players on my team? If so why? How will I know?

- Am I planning my company's day out before it begins? If not, why not?

Part 2 – Creating your plan

- Is there a way to create a strategy that costs less money, yet still solves a core issue?

- What specific things do I have to do each day/week/month?

- What deliverables are due by what dates?

- What are the monthly targets? Are they linear or progressive?

- Do I have absolute clarity on what is expected from each team member to implement this plan?

- What are the milestones I need to reach to know if my company is on track?

Plan, do, study, act (PDSA)

Plan: What am I going to do for the week? I want everything planned: I do not want to try working things in if the day goes well. The day revolves around these actions. Without these actions I don't hit my plan. If I don't hit my plan, something bad happens. When something bad happens, it causes other things to go wrong. This makes it harder to follow my plan. This makes it harder to plan how to recover the actions I should have done in the first place

Do: This is the work I must do each week. If it is on your profit goal list, it is non-negotiable.

Study: Review the numbers, how did we do? Do I have consequences, or can I celebrate?

Act: Keep doing the list or dispose of the list.

Playbook - What is your #1 Profit Goal?
When will it be due?
Who will be accountable?
Where will this business activity take place?
Why did you pick this goal?
How will the plan be executed?

Mini Target 1
Due Date:
Mini Target 2
Due Date:
Mini Target 3
Due Date:
Specific actions I will take Monthly:
Specific actions I will take weekly:

Specific actions I will take daily:
If not me, who will do this work?
The numbers I am going to track to measure my progress:
The day and time I will review my performance numbers:

What will happen if I miss my numbers during the week?
What will happen if I make my numbers during the week?
Does this plan take the most efficient route from the starting line to the finish line?
Did you hit your profit goal?
Why or why not?

What will you continue doing?
What will you stop doing?

Playbook - What is your #2 Profit Goal?
When will it be due?
Who will be accountable?
Where will this business activity take place?
Why did you pick this goal?
How will the plan be executed?

Mini Target 1
Due Date:
Mini Target 2
Due Date:
Mini Target 3
Due Date:
Specific actions I will take Monthly:
Specific actions I will take weekly:
Specific actions I will take daily:

If not me, who will do this work?
The numbers I am going to track to measure my progress:
The day and time I will review my performance numbers:
What will happen if I miss my numbers during the week?

What will happen if I make my numbers during the week?
Does this plan take the most efficient route from the starting line to the finish line?
Did you hit your profit goal?
Why or why not?

What will you continue doing?
What will you stop doing?

Playbook - What is your #3 Profit Goal?
When will it be due?
Who will be accountable?
Where will this business activity take place?
Why did you pick this goal?
How will the plan be executed?

Mini Target 1
Due Date:
Mini Target 2
Due Date:
Mini Target 3
Due Date:
Specific actions I will take Monthly:
Specific actions I will take weekly:
Specific actions I will take daily:

If not me, who will do this work?
The numbers I am going to track to measure my progress:
The day and time I will review my performance numbers:
What will happen if I miss my numbers during the week?
What will happen if I make my numbers during the week?

Does this plan take the most efficient route from the starting line to the finish line?
Did you hit your profit goal?
Why or why not?

What will you continue doing?
What will you stop doing?

Part 3 – Reflecting on the plan

- How much time am I investing each day in thinking about my playbook?

- Do I have a specific plan for my goal, or will I just hope I get there? Will inspect whether I achieve my goal or not?

- Can I execute this plan with the resources I have?

- Have I invested enough time challenging this plan and its timeline for completion (leaving behind the wishful-thinking, business-owner zone)?

- Do I have the skills to execute my part of the plan? Does my team? If not, is acquiring these skills included in the plan?

- Do I have a strategy-filled plan that outlines how I will break through my business hurdles?

- How much money is needed to implement this plan?

- What level of manpower is required to implement this plan?

- Is a change in the team line-up required?

Final Thoughts

Let's stop looking for the magic goals. The magic goal on your yearly plan will not solve your core issues. We need to get better at setting daily, weekly, and monthly requirements that must be completed, or our businesses will fail, and we will only have ourselves to blame.

Are we falling in love with the big ideal, instead of falling in love with the routine that, while not exciting, will lead us to those dreams? Let's get excited about the routine tasks: "I made ten customer calls today", "I invested half an hour thinking about customer referrals", and so on.

"Rainmakers answer the question, why should that customer do business with us? and then they go for it."

— Jeffrey Fox, *How To Become A Rainmaker*

Chapter 7 – Accountability and Execution

"What gets measured gets done."

— **Gino Wickman,** ***Traction: Get a Grip on Your Business***

Part 1 – Execution

- What are my most important activities?

- What am I going to measure to know if the plan was a success?

- Can the plan from Chapter 6 be executed by the team? Does the team want to consistently execute the plan? If not, the plan won't work.

- Am I falling in love with the vision, or the routine tasks that need to be completed to achieve the vision?

- If I do not tolerate poor financial leverage, why would I tolerate poor human-resource leverage?

- How much time each day do I invest thinking about accountability and execution?

- Now that I have adjusted the playbook, have I adjusted the resources to ensure the company can make the right plays?

- What can my staff and I cut back on doing, to make time for the things in the playbook that we need to do?

- What non-negotiable tasks need to happen in my business?

Part 2- Accountability

- What difficult conversations are needed, in order to fix the mistakes of the past?

- Am I accepting accountability, or am I constantly making excuses?

- Who are my accountability partners?

- Who on my team is lacking the discipline to complete the non-negotiable tasks?

- How frequently do I need to review our numbers?

- Who is accountable for each separate outcome in the playbook?

- Where are the inconsistencies in my team's execution? Why? What are the core issues or hurdles?

- Are my employees taking ownership of their work?

- Are my employees accountable for measurable results that are inspected on a regular basis?

- Do I have the courage, as a manager or owner, to have the difficult conversations with employees that are required? If not, why not?

Final Thoughts

There are only two reasons your plan will not work:

- It is the wrong plan;
- It has been poorly executed.

When something goes wrong, or your business is struggling, one of two things has happened:

- Something you thought was going to happen did not happen;
- Something you did not think was going to happen happened.

For your plan to succeed, it is imperative that you know your business' three most important non-negotiable tasks. If you can't pick three, or you do not have the discipline to stick to them, please, stop now and give this book to someone else.

Do not delay the difficult conversations with team members, they need to happen.

"Remember, having a C or B team in your company for leverage is like having a high interest adjustable loan for your financial leverage."

– Max Keller

Monthly Accountability Net Profit Call Framework

Welcome to the Monthly Net Profit Call. This call is only for business owners who are serious about hitting their net profit goals. **The desired outcome of the call is for members to make increased net profit through accountability, clarity, and consistency.**

Rules for the call

1. We will always start and end on time. We cannot find more time, if you are late to register for a call.
2. Unplug from your other tasks and devices: Engage.
3. The call will be up to, but not longer than, one hour.
4. Everyone will have a couple of minutes to go through the questions with the host: Keep your answers brief and to the point.
5. For most of the call, someone else will be talking: Use this as a time to listen and learn about what is working for others and how it could benefit you.
6. Everyone on the call will agree to take absolute accountability for what happens in their business: No excuses.
7. Everyone on the call will be prepared to answer the following questions.
8. Participating in this call means you need to be focused and ready to do whatever it takes to achieve your profit numbers.

Questions for each member need to think about before the call:

1. What is the profit goal you are currently working on?
2. What is the due date?
3. What is the mini-goal and due date?
4. What is your most important monthly activity, weekly activity, and daily activity?
5. What will happen if you do not achieve your goals?
6. What potential hurdles could keep you from reaching your goals?
7. Are you on track to achieve your goals?
8. What are you measuring to assess whether you are on track to achieve your goals?

Want to join our Net Profit Calls? Reach out to us at www.customerschasingyou.com, info@saviorpublishinghouse.com, or 817-527-8207 to sign up.

Book List – Additional Reading

Cardone, G. (2011). *The Ten Times Rule: The Only Difference Between Success and Failure.* Hoboken, NJ: Wiley.

Cunningham, K. J. (2018). *The Road Less Stupid: Advice from the Chairman of the Board.* Austin, TX: Keys to the Vault.

DeMarco, M. (2011). *The Millionaire Fastlane: Crack the Code to Wealth and Live Rich for a Lifetime.* Phoenix, AZ: Viperion Publishing Corporation.

Fox, J. J. (2015). *How to Become a Rainmaker: The Rules for Getting and Keeping Customers and Clients.* New York: Hachette Books.

Gerber, M. E. (2009). *E-Myth Mastery: The Seven Essential Disciplines for Building a World Class Company*. New York: HarperCollins e-books.

Godin, S. (2018). *Linchpin: Are you Indispensable?* London: Piatkus.

Hill, N. H. (2016). *Think and Grow Rich*. Place of publication not identified: Ben Holden-Crowther.

Hyatt, M. (2018). *Your Best Year Ever: A 5-Step Plan for Achieving Your Most Important Goals.* Grand Rapids, MI: Baker Books, a division of Baker Publishing Group.

Keller, G., & Papasan, J. (2017). *The One Thing: The Surprisingly Simple Truth Behind Extraordinary Results*. Austin, TX: Bard Press.

McKeown, G. (2014). *Essentialism: The Disciplined Pursuit of Less*. London: Virgin.

Newport, C. (2016). *Deep Work*. London: Piatkus.

Schroeder, A. (2010). *The Snowball: Warren Buffett and the Business of Life*. London: Bloomsbury Paperbacks.

Scott, S. (2006). *The Richest Man Who Ever Lived: King Solomon's Secrets to Success, Wealth, and Happiness*. New York: Currency/Doubleday.

Wickman, G. (2012). *Traction.* Place of publication not identified: Benbella Books.

About Max Keller

As Max reached year end in his real estate investment business, he was happy with his deal activity but was not happy with the profits. Max wondered why after so much work there was not more left at the end of the year. This search for answers led to finding a profit consultant, consulting others, and now the creation of this book. Max believes the best gift you can give your company is more net profit. Max is on a daily journey to help his companies and his client's companies be as profitable as possible.

Max earned his B.B.A. in Finance from The University of Texas at Austin and his M.A. in Teaching from Louisiana College. He has over 15 years of experience in real estate, finance, and teaching. A few of his current roles are consultant, teacher, author, speaker, and expert panelist.

Max created Savior Publishing House as a way to help real estate businesses attract more customers and become more profitable. The Savior brand of companies focuses on providing Christian real estate and business solutions to our clients. Max enjoys spending time with his wife and children and engaging in family activities, such as being involved at church and going on vacation. He is passionate about investing time in his family.

Notes:

Notes:

Notes:

Notes:

Notes:

Notes:

Notes:

Notes:

Notes:

Notes:

Notes:

Notes:

Notes:

Notes:

$97.00
ISBN 978-1-7338459-7-7
59700>
9 781733 845977

Made in the USA
Middletown, DE
05 November 2026

36552533R10057